THE IWCR CONSTITUTION *APPROVED*

IPOTI WEALTH CREATION REUNION

THE CONSTITUTION OF IPOTI WEALTH CREATION REUNION

ARTICLE I

Name.

The name of the organization shall be "IPOTI WEALTH CREATION REUNION". The original letters of "IEWCR" shall identify the association. It shall be a nonpolitical movement organized to awake Ipotians to the development of Ipoti - Ekiti community.

ARTICLE II

Aims & Objectives.

2.1 To wake up the indegenes of the community to their responsibilities to the   town.

2.2 To promote a better development and beautification of our hometown, Ipoti Ekiti, Nigeria.

2.3 To encourage and promote social interactions among members.

2.4 To bring our children closer together so that they recognize themselves as indigenes of Ipoti Ekiti.

2.5 To create future values for our youths by guiding them in areas of education, skills and employment programs to assure a quality standard of living at old age.

2.6 To provide moral, financial and material supports to Ipotians in Nigeria and all over the world whenever the needs arise.

2. To promote the welfare of members

2.8 To support, liaise and cooperate with any individuals organizations or governmental Agencies in any programs and activities that are geared toward the progress and development of Ipoti community.

2.9 To act as a pressure Group and intellectual Round- Table,advocating for Rapid development and good governance of Ipoti community.

ARTICLE III

MEMBERSHIP

3.1 Membership shall be open to:

a. All sons and daughters of Ipoti - Ekiti (either by maternal or paternal right) and their spouses.

b. All other persons who do not qualify under clause 3.1 (a] above but who have been residents of lpoti - Ekiti for a period of three years or more and who   are seen to have genuine interest in the progress and development of lpoti   community .

3.2 All prospective members must be at least 21 years of age.

3.3 There shall be two categories of membership;

a. STUDENT MEMBERSHIP

Subject to the provisions of the clauses 3.1(a) and 3. I (b) above, any person who is registered or attending a tertiary institution of learning or a vocational institute shall be registered as a student member with annual dues waiver. However, such person shall be converted into a regularmember upon completion of an educational program or on securing employment.

b. FINANCIAL MEMBERS

(1.) Subject to the provisions of clauses 3.1(a) (b) and 3.2 above, a person may be registered as a financial member. Such a person must be financially viable to pay the membership dues and any monetary contributions that may be levied to maintain the Group.(2) To be considered a financial member one must be up to date in paying dues and must participate in meetings regularly.

3.4 Open membership- No formal application may be filled to become a member

ARTICLE IV

TERMINATION OF MEMBERSHIP

Any membership that acts in a way which is considered detrimental (as defined by the Group) to the interest of the Group shall be issued two warnings by the Group. If a third offence occurs,such a member shall be expelled by a vote of the majority of members participating in such deliberation

ARTICLE V

The following Offices shall be established for the smooth functioning of the group:

(1) Chairman

(2) Vice Chairman

(3) General Secretary

(4) Treasurer

(5) Financial Secretary

(6) Social! Publicity Secretary

(7) Patrons and Matrons

Duties of the officers

(A) The Chairman:

(1) Shall preside over all meetings

(2) Shall be the spokesperson for the Group.

(3) Shall have the power to delegate duties for the smooth operation of the Group.

(4) Shall convey emergency meetings as needed.

(5) Shall co-ordinate the activities of various committees of the Group.

(6) Shall submit an annual report on the activities of the Group. Such a report must be reflecting the activities of the Group for the year (as may be determined by the Group)

(B) The Vice-Chairman.

(1) In the absence of the Chairman, the vice Chairman shall assume the official duties of the chairman.

(2) Shall perform any other functions as may be assigned to him/ her by either the chairman or the Group.

(C) The General Secretary

(1) Shall serve as the secretary of the Group.

(3) Shall be responsible for all the official correspondence of the Group

(3) Shall maintain accurate records of all the procedures of the Group's meetings.

(4) Shall notify all members as to the time and place of the regular and special meetings of the Group.

(D) The Treasurer

(1) Shall be in charge of all the funds of the Group.

(2) Shall deposit the monies paid to him/her in the designated group's account within five working days from the date of receipt of such monies from the financial secretary, unless the group decides otherwise.

(F) Social Publicity Secretary

(1) Shall be responsible for publicizing the activities of the Group. Such activities shall be in collaboration with the executive committee and as approved by the house.

(G) Patrons and Matrons

The Group may, from time to time appoint persons as patrons and matrons who have rendered exceptional and meritorious services in our community. Their duration of office shall be determined by the Group. Such appointees shall be by a nomination and final voting approved by the general meeting of the house.

ARTICLE VI VARIOUS COMMITTEES

The following committees shall be established for the Group: 1. Constitution Drafting / Legal services Committee.

2. Youth Development and Education Committee

3. Fund Raising and Development Committee

4. Infrastructural Committee

5. Five Super Committee

FUNCTIONS

1. Constitutional Drafting / Legal Services Committee…

(i) Review the constitution of the Group from time to time as may be recommended by the general house for necessary amendments.

(ii) Provide legal supports and advice to the group.

(iii) Carry out any other functions as may be assigned by the general house.

2) Youth Development and Education Committee..

1. To devise means of organizing programs that will connect our [ipoti] youths to job training opportunities ,career instructions, after school programs, academic improvements, financial literacy training and social growth.

2. To encourage youth empowerment by helping ipoti youths to discover, develop, and achieve their skills and talents.

3. To identify means of awarding scholarships and other financial Aids to Ipoti students ,based on either academic performances, or financial needs.

4. To identify areas in need of renovation of class rooms and buildings in our existing schools at Ipoti.

   Provision of and renovation of equipment of computers and internet services in our community public institutions.

5. To advocate for the establishment of higher institutions and industries in our community.

6. The provision of school supplies.

7. The committee, in the performance of any of the above functions shall always recommend its findings to the General house for a review and final approval

3. Fund Raising and Development Committee.

1. To Come Up With Methods of raising funds for the administrative operations of the Group.

2. To Identity areas of strategic development needs in the town.

3. To develop strategies for raising funds for development efforts.

4. To develop processes and procedures for financial operations of the group including but not limited to : Account Operating procedures, Fund collection procedures, Disbursement procedures and. Control over financial operations etc.

5. To lead in process of contacting individuals and corporations that can fund the groups development efforts

6. To cooperate with other groups with similar goals in the town for good coordination so that duplication in fund raising is avoided.

7. To perform any other duties relating to its area of jurisdiction as directed by the board

8. To spearhead the operational set-up of the group such as incorporation and account opening etc.

4. Infrastructural Committee

I. To identify, evaluate and recommend to the Group for appropriate actions, conditions of existing infrastructural facilities in the Town such as:

a) Electrical power systems

b) Water supply systems

c) Telecommunications

d) Transportation

e) Banking and Finance.

f) Emergency services [including medical, ;police ;Fire and rescue]

g) To organize waste disposal system and maintaining city water drainage system

h) Public institutions [post offices; Hospitals; and Libraries]

2. To search for and recommend to the Group other infrastructures that can speed up development and attract people to visit or love to reside in the community.

3. To supervise and conduct a periodic review of the states of and the efficiency of the existing infrastructures and report findings to the Group for a follow up.

5. Five members Super committee..

(i) It shall also be known as the Disciplinary Committee

(ii) It shall be headed by the Chairman of the Group and four other members drawn from other existing committees.

(iii) Shall have the power to investigate any allegation of impropriety against any officer or committee and recommend his / her dismissal, or the dissolution of such committee.

(iv) A member of the Super Committee who is being investigated shall not sit in the Super Committees investigational deliberations.

Article VII

Elections

1 The Election of Group officers shall be held every four years on the last Sunday of December or any other day and date as may be approve by the general house.

2. The house shall approve of electoral body.

3. Nomination of officers for the general election shall be held on the day of the Election.

4. All active members shall be eligible to vote and be voted for in all elections of the Group

5. All Officers shall be elected through simple majority vote by an open ballot.

6 Officers may be elected in absentia.

7 The outgoing executive shall surrender all Group property to the new administration within four weeks after election.

B. DURATION OF TERMS IN OFFICE

 No officer shall serve more than two terms in the same office consequently.

C. REMOVAL FROM OFFICE

Any officer who fails to perform his / her duties adequately, or Commits an act detrimental to the progress of the group may be requested to relinquish the office by the Group during his / her term in office. Such removal shall be at the instance of two thirds of the house voting a particular meeting subject to the provisions of the article VI(5) (III)

ARTICLE VIll

Income & Finances

1. The Group Shall derive its funds from :

A. membership subscription! Annual Dues.

B. Donations and gifts.

C. Fund raising.

D. Special levies.

E. Proceeds From the Group properties.

F. Any other suggested means.

2. Any reputable bank[s] shall be chosen for the deposits of the Groups funds. The signatories to the Group account shall be at least any two of the following.

A. President.

B. Financial Secretary.

C. Treasurer.

3. The General house must approve all the Groups Expenditures' Beyond --
#100,000.00[one hundred thousand naira] or its foreign equivalent.

4. The Executive Committee may approve any expenses up to -100,000.00 naira[or its
foreign equivalent]

ARTICLE IX

1 There shall be at least 12 General Meetings within a Year

2. General Meetings shall commenced at the date and time agreed upon by the majority
of the members of the Group.

3. The General Meetings shall be The "Supreme Council" Of The Group.

4. At the discretion of the executive committee the chairman may call

   emergency meetings.

5. Simple majority of the active members shall form a quorum

ARTICLE X

Constitution Amendments Implementation and Review.

A Amendments.

Amendments to This Constitution shall be Submitted to the Chairman in writing. It Shall be discussed and then voted on by the simple majority of the house and then submitted to the constitution draft committee for implementation.

B. Implementation

This Constitution Shall be implemented and go into effect Immediately.

C. Review

This Constitution Shall be Subject to review Every 3 Years

BARR. IDOWU 0 JEGEDE, Esquire.

****

THE EXECUTIVES POSTS (ELECTIVE OFFICES)

****

1) CHAIRMAN OF THE REUNION -

2) VICE. CHAIRMAN OF THE REUNION -

3) G.SECRETARY OF THE REUNION -

4) FINANCE SECRETARY OF THE REUNION-

5) PRO. SECRETARY OF THE REUNION-

APPROVED / PATRON AND MATRON POSTS

1) PATRON -

2) PATRON -

1) MATRON-

2) MATRON-

COMMITTEE CHAIRMEN AND THEIR SECRETARY POSTS

JOIN ANY COMMITTEE OF YOUR CHOICE CONSIDERING YOUR FIELD OF SPECIALIZATION.

1) CONSTITUTION DRAFTING COMMITTEE.

CHAIRMAN –

SECRETARY -

****

2) FUND RAISING COMMITTEE.

CHAIRMAN –

SECRETARY –

3) YOUTH AND SOCIAL DEVELOPMENT COMMITTEE.

    CHAIRMAN –

    SECRETARY -

****

4) DEVELOPMENT / INFRASTRUCTURAL PLAN COMMITTEES.

    CHAIRMAN –

    SECRETARY –

****

5) FIVE MAN SUPER COMMITTEE (DISPLINARY COMMITTEE)

1) ----------------------

2) ---------------------

3) ---------------------

4) ---------------------

5) CHAIRMAN OF THE REUNION (MEMBER)

Constitution Drafting Committee

1. Caleb Arogundade Esquire.

2. Idowu O. Jegede Esquire.

UNITED WE STAND

LONG LIVE IPOTI, OUR PRIDE

Printed by.. F& F resources (Nig. Ltd) a. Sub. of Nigit Consultants. Italy.

Website. www.fandfresources.com